D1606794

The Meltdown at Three Mile Island

Published in 2003 by The Rosen Publishing Group, Inc.
29 East 21st Street, New York, NY 10010

Library of Congress Cataloging-in-Publication Data

Derkins, Susie.
The meltdown at Three Mile Island / Susie Derkins. — 1st ed.
p. cm. — (When disaster strikes!)
Summary: Presents an overview of how nuclear power plants function, the history of nuclear energy use in the United States, and describes the nuclear accident at the Three Mile Island Nuclear Power Plant in Pennsylvania and the aftermath of that disaster.
Includes bibliographical references and index.
ISBN 0-8239-3678-3 (library binding)
1. Three Mile Island Nuclear Power Plant—Juvenile literature. 2. Nuclear power plants—Accidents—Pennsylvania—Harrisburg Region—Juvenile literature.
[1. Three Mile Island Nuclear Power Plant. 2. Nuclear power plants—Accidents.
3. Nuclear energy.]
I. Title. II. When disaster strikes! (New York, N.Y.)
TK1345.H37 D47 2003
363.17'99'0974818—dc21
                                                                    2001008522

Manufactured in the United States of America

On the cover:
The cooling towers of the Three Mile Island nuclear power plant spew steam after the 1979 accident.

Contents

A year after the accident at Three Mile Island, people protest the nuclear power plant's continued operation.

Introduction

On March 28, 1979, the
United States experienced a major
nuclear accident. In the early morning
hours of that Wednesday, two water
pumps in the cooling system at Three
Mile Island (TMI), a large nuclear
power plant in the small northeastern
city of Harrisburg, Pennsylvania,
simply stopped operating. Although
the nuclear reactor's automatic safety
systems responded appropriately
to this minor malfunction, TMI plant
operators did not. A series of errors
in the automated operating system
of the nuclear power plant and on
the part of plant staff resulted in the
worst nuclear accident in United
States history.

Had the situation not been brought under control in time, it may have led to one of the worst of all possible man-made disasters: total nuclear meltdown. Thankfully, no one was killed or even injured as a result of the Three Mile Island disaster. It did leave the power plant inoperable, however, and cost nearly $1 billion to clean up. More important, it had a serious and lasting effect on American nuclear energy policy and development.

Nuclear Power

Nuclear power is a way to create energy—in the form of heat—by processing radioactive elements such as uranium. This energy can then be used to fuel enormous power generators for things like lighting or heating homes and office buildings. Elements like uranium release charged particles when they disintegrate, causing a heat-producing reaction. (This process is described in more detail in chapter 1.)

One of the benefits of nuclear power is that, compared to earlier sources of electrical power, it is very "clean." Coal, for instance, was once relied upon to fire power plants and provide consumers with electricity. However, coal is very hazardous to the environment. Energy plants fueled by coal fires release large amounts of carbon and sulfur into the atmosphere, causing numerous health problems for people in coal-burning towns who breathe in the dirty air.

Nuclear energy has its environmental problems too, however. Mining uranium is not an environmentally clean process. It can result in the production of radioactive waste and pollution that damages the local environment and affects the health of mine workers. Transporting nuclear fuel to and from plants by train and trucks can also be very dangerous because of the risk of accidents that may result in leaks or spills.

Although every safety measure is taken to ensure that accidents will not happen, disasters still can and do occur. The Chernobyl meltdown in 1986 in the former Soviet Union sent 5 percent of the plant's radioactive core into the atmosphere, killed 30 people

This massive lot at the federal nuclear manufacturing site at Oak Ridge, Tennessee, is filled with drums holding hazardous nuclear waste. The atomic bomb that was dropped on Hiroshima, Japan, in World War II was developed at Oak Ridge.

Mike Pintek: Reporter

"We first learned that something was wrong at Three Mile Island because our traffic reporter . . . says 'You know, I'm getting things up on the scanners here. Are you picking this up? . . . Apparently they've mobilized some fire equipment and emergency people at Three Mile Island . . . Oh by the way, there's no steam coming out of the cooling towers.' So now I'm thinking, hmm, something really weird's going on there."

From *The American Experience: Meltdown at Three Mile Island*

(28 from radiation exposure), and caused 209 people to be treated for radioactive poisoning. Ten people later died of a thyroid cancer linked to nuclear fallout from the accident. Chernobyl remains the only accident in commercial nuclear history to result in fatalities.

These types of disasters inevitably lead to increased precautions and safety measures at power plants, and more thorough training of plant operators and technicians. Certainly, if the operators at Three Mile Island had properly responded to the system's malfunction, the crisis could have been avoided. Nuclear energy has inherent risks, however, even when the automated equipment, procedures, and employees are all top-notch. Even if nuclear energy is produced without mishap, the process that creates the energy also creates toxic waste products. Used nuclear fuel remains radioactive for centuries after its use. To this day, there is no method to dispose of or store used nuclear fuel in a way that is entirely safe.

The Deadly Power of Nuclear Fuel

At the time of the Three Mile Island disaster, most Americans were already familiar with the deadly potential of nuclear power. In August 1945, the United States initiated a nuclear attack on Japan in order to make the Japanese surrender and bring about the end of World War II. Two atomic bombs were dropped on Japan on the orders of U.S. president Harry S. Truman. The first atomic bomb was dropped on Hiroshima on August 6, 1945; the second, on the city of Nagasaki on August 9. The two attacks killed approximately 150,000 to 220,000 people within four months of the bombing, from building collapses, burns, and radiation exposure. Thousands more eventually died as a result of cancers caused by the radioactive poison that lingered in the atmosphere and environment for many years afterward.

The accident at Three Mile Island is still considered the most serious to have occurred in the United States and one of the worst nuclear accidents in history. Public concern over the TMI disaster brought about changes in the ways in which the government and the nuclear power industry planned for emergencies, trained their operators, and contained and disposed of radioactive materials. It also changed the way many people thought about potential energy sources and safety. In short, the TMI disaster forced the nuclear power industry and people all over the world to ask tough questions about technological progress and to focus continuously upon safety and health issues.

Despite the risks, Americans continue to rely on nuclear fuel for much of their energy needs. Little has been done to develop safer fuel alternatives, such as solar energy. Nuclear power currently provides about 17 percent of the world's electricity. Some countries depend more on nuclear power than others. According to figures published by the Nuclear Regulatory Commission and the Department of Energy, 77 percent of France's electricity is generated from nuclear power, while in the United States, nuclear power supplies only about 22 percent of the electricity. Nuclear power provides more than 50 percent of the total energy supply to six states. Worldwide, there are more than 434 nuclear power plants in more than thirty countries; 110 of those plants are located in the United States.

What exactly happened on that fateful day in Pennsylvania? How is nuclear power created, and why are people so reliant upon it? Given its dangers, why is it such a tempting source of energy? And what could the continued use of nuclear power—especially the reprocessed variety—mean in the future? Let's take a look at nuclear power and the ways in which its use and mishandling led to the Three Mile Island disaster.

1

What Is Nuclear Energy?

Each bit of matter is made of atoms, tiny particles that attach to each other to form molecules. Certain combinations of atoms form more than 100 types of matter—including air and gases—known as elements. About a century ago, scientists learned that the atoms of certain elements, such as uranium, are radioactive. That means that they give off charged particles when they disintegrate, or break apart, causing heat-producing reactions. It was discovered that enormous amounts of energy were released when uranium atoms were split. This energy could be captured, stored, and harnessed as power.

How a Nuclear Reactor Works

Every nuclear power generator contains a radioactive core that acts as a heat-producing furnace. Within the core, uranium atoms are split again and again in order to generate heat, thereby producing energy. To control the speed at which atoms split and produce heat, control rods are lowered into or raised out of the core. Lowering the rods slows the reaction and keeps temperatures fairly consistent; raising the rods increases the reaction, and raises the core's temperature.

Primary Loop

Water, flowing from a reactor's primary loop through a complicated system of valves and pumps, swirls around the core. This circulation of water is also used for temperature control: Water absorbs the excess heat generated by the control rods. Various types of pumps and valves keep the water flowing through the reactor's primary loop. One of these is a pilot-operated release valve, or PORV. This is an escape valve for the steam that builds as water grows hotter. Without it, the pressure and heat created by the steam would build to dangerous levels.

Another type of pump is an emergency injection water pump, or EIW. The EIW is a backup mechanism. It allows additional water—or, in an emergency, special nuclear coolant—to enter the system when a malfunction results in a shortage of water. Without coolant, the reactor can overheat and cause a dangerous accident. The addition of cool water can help to reduce the system's temperature and avoid having to resort to the more drastic use of chemical nuclear coolant.

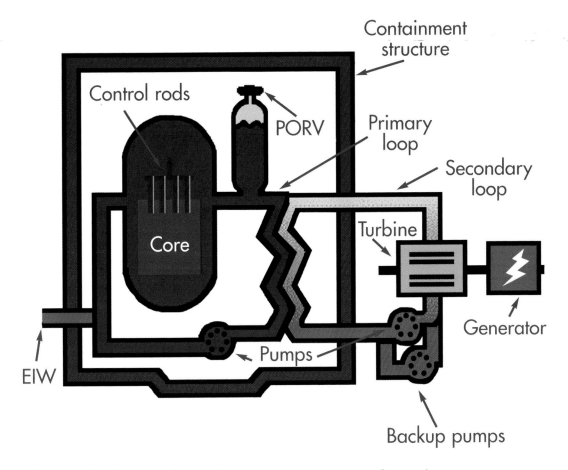

This simple diagram shows the various components of a nuclear reactor.

Because the water and coolants swirl around the nuclear reactor's radioactive core, they too become radioactive. Therefore, a nuclear reactor's core and most of its primary loop are surrounded by containment walls made of solid concrete, several feet thick. These walls act as a barrier, so that harmful radioactive energy given off by the core, valves, and coolant cannot escape into the atmosphere.

Wednesday, March 28

4:00 AM

Pumps in the secondary cooling circuit stop operating, leading to increased pressure in the primary cooling circuit and automatic shutdown.

Secondary Loop

Heat that is generated in the nuclear core's primary loop is transferred by water to another location: the reactor's secondary loop. This water is so hot that in the secondary loop it turns to steam, which is the mist that water becomes after being heated to its boiling point. The steam powers a turbine, or engine. Once the turbine has been powered by the secondary core's steam, it transfers this energy to a power generator, which in turn produces electricity.

How Did We Come to Rely on Nuclear Energy?

Interest in using nuclear technology to produce energy was first sparked in the aftermath of World War II. In 1946, after the United States's attack on Japan, President Harry S. Truman signed the Atomic Energy Act. The act allowed the developing nuclear energy industry to be controlled not by the government, but by civilians—ordinary businesspeople and other private individuals. At the same time, Truman established a congressional committee on atomic energy. Known as the Atomic Energy Commission, its purpose was to monitor the growth and activities of the nuclear power industry—to be a sort of official "watchdog." At the time, this commission was thought to be enough to exercise control over the responsible functioning of nuclear power plants. The Atomic Energy Commission's first official assignment began in 1947, when it set out to investigate how nuclear energy could be harnessed for peaceful uses. In 1955, the commission announced the creation of an agreement between the U.S. government and the nuclear power industry to jointly develop nuclear power plants.

America's First Nuclear Power Plants

The first to benefit from this new agreement was the tiny town of Arco, Idaho, which at that time had a population of only 1,200. Arco became the first town in the United States to have its power come from a nuclear energy source—the Borax III, a boiling-water reactor still in an early stage of development. Similar "experimental" reactors that were built around this time were already beginning to malfunction. In Idaho Falls, another small town about fifty miles west of Arco, a new reactor called the SL-1 partially melted down during a routine test in November 1955. The cause of the accident was ultimately blamed on operator error. Fortunately, no one was hurt, but it was clear that this early technology was hardly foolproof.

Nevertheless, the creation of new power plants continued full speed ahead. In December 1957, the first full-scale nuclear power plant in the United States was built in Shippingport, Pennsylvania. Unlike the small-scale, "experimental" plants in Idaho, the Pennsylvania plant was able to generate enough electricity to reach its full generating capacity after only three weeks of activity. Soon, nuclear power plants were popping up all across the land. By 1959, nuclear power plants, such as the Dresden 1 Nuclear Power Station in Illinois, were being built without any financial help from the United States government. The industry was booming.

Clinton Anderson (left), chairman of the Joint Congressional Committee on Atomic Energy, and Atomic Energy Commission chairman Lewis L. Strauss view a photograph of the United States's first full-scale atomic energy power plant under construction in Shippingport, Pennsylvania, in May 1956.

By the early 1960s, nuclear power plants were being built in towns that could hardly be considered remote. In late 1963, the Atomic Energy Commission accepted the Jersey Central Power and Light Company's (JCPL) proposal to build the huge Oyster Creek nuclear power plant in Forked River, New Jersey, fifty miles north of Atlantic City. Oyster Creek would provide an alternative to expensive fossil-fuel energy for residents of densely populated central New Jersey. In late 1966, an experimental reactor near Detroit, Michigan, known as the Enrico Fermi plant—named for the Nobel Prize–winning Italian physicist who developed the first nuclear reactor in 1942—saw its core partially melt. Although a deadly reaction was prevented in time, the Fermi reactor was damaged badly enough that its core was permanently disabled.

War in Far-off Lands

These early accidents should have been treated as warning signs of potentially more catastrophic disasters. Yet despite several frightening close calls, nuclear power plants continued to be built and operated all across the United States and elsewhere in the world. Power outages, such as the famous electrical blackout of the northeastern United States in November 1965, prompted the government and energy industry to strongly consider alternative energy sources, such as nuclear power.

In addition, an energy crisis developed in the mid-1970s as a result of an international conflict between Israel and various oil-producing Arab states. Several of these countries came together to

Wednesday, March 28

4:02 AM

After a pressure relief valve fails to close, steam generators boil dry and the core begins to overheat.

form the Organization of Petroleum Exporting Countries (OPEC), a trade group that would decide how much oil to export and at what price. Intent on retaliating against Israel and its allies, including the United States, OPEC quickly reduced oil supplies and raised prices. Gasoline prices skyrocketed as supply decreased; between 1972 and 1979, the price of oil increased from three dollars a barrel to thirty dollars a barrel. Eventually, oil became so scarce in the United States that it was available only on a rationed basis. Incredibly long lines could be found at gas stations across the country as people waited for several hours to get their tanks filled. The energy crisis further increased interest in alternative energy sources that were cheap and could be developed in the United States, rather than imported from other countries (as in the case with oil).

Motorists line up at a gas station on Long Island, New York, hoping to fill their tanks during the gasoline shortage of 1973–1974. Long lines at gas pumps and fuel restrictions were common across the United States during the shortage.

Quickly Turning to Nuclear Fuel

To address these immediate energy supply problems, President Gerald Ford abolished President Truman's Atomic Energy Commission in 1974 and replaced it with two new governmental bodies that would closely monitor the energy industry. The first was the Energy Research and Development Administration, which was responsible for streamlining the federal government's nuclear energy research and development—for technological, "peaceful" needs as well as those related to defense—within one unified agency. The second body was the Nuclear Regulatory Commission (NRC), which was responsible for regulating the actions of the nuclear power industry. The creation of the two new governmental bodies signaled a serious commitment to the advancement of nuclear power.

Robin Neenan Stuart: Harrisburg, PA, Resident

"It was a beautiful day. A very sunny, bright morning. My windows were open. My phone rang, and my sister wanted to know where I was going. She was calling from L.A., saying, 'Get out! Get out! Hurry up and get out!' And people around the country were calling and saying, you know, 'Get out of there! Hurry up and get out!'"

From *The American Experience: Meltdown at Three Mile Island*

Downtown Middletown, Pennsylvania, offers a clear view of the cooling towers of the Three Mile Island nuclear power plant.

America's new focus on nuclear energy may have eased energy shortage problems in the short term, but the nuclear power industry continued to play with fire. President Jimmy Carter, who was inaugurated in 1977, was one of the few who spoke of the potential dangers of heavy reliance on nuclear power and the desire for profit that often accompanied it. But power plants continued to be built—including a large plant in Harrisburg, Pennsylvania, named Three Mile Island—with very few public declarations of concern. This silence would soon be shattered.

2

The Birth and Death of Three Mile Island

In September 1978, a dedication ceremony was held for the recently completed Three Mile Island nuclear power plant in Harrisburg, Pennsylvania. Three Mile Island was a huge plant. Its radioactive core was built to be twelve feet long, weighing 100 tons. At full capacity, it could produce enough energy to light more than 18,000 homes.

At the ceremony, John F. O'Leary, deputy secretary of energy for the Carter administration, boasted that nuclear power was a "bright and shining option" to provide energy for the United States.

He described the plant as a success in America's plan to move away from its dependency on oil imported from foreign—and often hostile—countries. The plant would provide not just energy but also jobs to the people of Harrisburg. Everything seemed golden. But a mere six months later, in March 1979, Three Mile Island was the site of the worst nuclear accident in U.S. history.

What happened on that fateful day in Harrisburg? Let's detail what happened to the system that ran Three Mile Island, step by step.

The Malfunction at TMI

On Wednesday, March 28, 1979, beginning at approximately 4 AM, water pumps in the secondary loop of Three Mile Island's core reactor shut down as a result of a minor malfunction. (Three Mile Island had two core reactors, TMI-1 and TMI-2. The 1979 disaster took place at TMI-2; TMI-1 was unaffected by the accident. Here, we will just refer to the site of the disaster as TMI.) A warning alarm went off in the TMI control room. Since the pumps were not active, heat was no longer being transferred to the secondary loop. Water began to back up and pressurize in the primary loop, and as a result, the temperature there increased.

To alleviate this backup of heated water, the reactor's pilot-operated relief valve (PORV) opened automatically, as it should have done. Heat, in the form of pressurized steam, was safely released into a holding tank. At this point, the situation was a minor malfunction that was properly corrected by the system's automatic safety functions. The problem should have ended here, with the crisis safely and correctly averted.

Victor Stello: NRC Senior Engineer

"I went to mass, and I was real, real tired. I thought I was gonna fall asleep in the sermon. And then this priest gets up and said that because of the potential for us being killed from Three Mile Island, we're going to have general absolution [usually reserved for people going into battle and who are likely to be killed]."

**From *The American Experience:
Meltdown at Three Mile Island***

Less than two minutes after this initial malfunction, however, a grave occurrence took place: The PORV should have closed after it released the steam that had built up in the primary loop, but it became stuck open. The PORV has a warning light. When it switches on, the PORV valves are open; when the light is out, the PORV valves are closed. When the Three Mile Island operators checked the PORV light, it was out—but in reality, the indicator light was malfunctioning. As a result, the operators thought the PORV was closed and functioning properly when it was not. This valve had malfunctioned eleven times before in other nuclear plants, but nothing had been done by TMI's operators or the NRC to anticipate or correct the problem.

Without the operators' knowledge, steam and hot water continued to flow through the mistakenly open valve, resulting in a loss of cooling water in the reactor core. Another backup safety mechanism was automatically activated: emergency injection water, or

Wednesday, March 28

4:03 AM

Emergency core cooling system begins pumping water into the overheating core, but an operator mistakenly reduces the flow of coolant.

EIW. Cool water flowed into the primary loop to cool down the dangerous buildup of excessive heat caused by the open valve and the loss of coolant. TMI operators believed that the pumps were responding correctly, given that the PORV light indicated that the valve was closed.

Three Mile Island operators believed they had no cause for alarm at this point. The EIW system activating automatically was not unusual; TMI technicians had seen the EIW kick into action before. About five minutes after the initial malfunction, the TMI operators shut off the EIW, believing that the secondary loop's water levels were rising as they should and therefore cooling the system adequately.

However, the water levels in the secondary loop were actually dropping. The water, along with a dangerous amount of pressurized steam, was instead continuing to back up in the PORV. Nearly 3,000 gallons of radioactive water escaped from the primary loop before a TMI operator finally noticed that the valves for the backup pumps in the secondary loop had been shut down. This operator opened the valves, believing that it would restore the normal flow of water through the secondary loop and reduce the temperature and pressure in the reactor's core.

Malfunctions continued to occur, however, and caused new problems even as the TMI operators tried to address the earlier errors. A tremendous amount of hot steam and water had accumulated in the PORV. Under normal circumstances, the pumps should have been able to force the steam

This undated photo shows engineers inside the control room of the Three Mile Island nuclear plant prior to the accident on March 28, 1979.

and water through the system. But since the backup was so great, the pumps began to vibrate instead. Noticing this, TMI operators shut down two of the four pumps. As a result, the steam in the primary loop increased—and water circulation decreased—even more. Without water circulation, the reactor's core became even hotter. A lack of water flow through the pumps converted more of the water into extremely hot and pressurized steam.

Wednesday, March 28

5:00 AM

Pumps in the primary cooling circuit begin to vibrate and are shut down. The reactor core's temperature rises even further.

Second Shift

Nearly two and a half hours after the initial malfunction, an operator who had recently arrived for his morning shift noticed that the temperature of steam being leaked from the PORV was abnormally high. To correct this, he shut off the PORV backup valve. But he and other operators were still failing to realize that the water level in the primary loop was dangerously low. Water must cover the entire reactor core to prevent overheating and explosion of the control rods. Once the water level in the primary loop of the TMI reactor dipped below the top of the core, the steam became superheated, and the control rods began to release hydrogen and radioactive gases. So much water had drained away that half the core was uncovered, and the radioactivity of the water in the primary loop was 350 times the normal level. Temperatures in the reactor were reaching 4,300 degrees; core meltdown usually occurs at 5,200 degrees.

Piercing radiation alarms began to go off and control panels were blinking furiously; the operators announced that Three Mile Island was in an official state of emergency. TMI operators finally recognized that the pressure relief valve had been open, and so they closed it—far too late to make a difference, however. A valve that should have closed automatically after a few seconds remained open for almost two and a half hours because of human operators misreading the system's signals.

More than seven and a half hours after the initial malfunction, operators attempted to lower the system's temperature by pumping cool, nonradioactive water through the PORV. Nevertheless, the pressure remained at a dangerous level. Once again, the TMI system's backup valve opened to release the pressure. But instead, the hydrogen and radioactive gases—released by the control rods and leaked into the system via the open pressure release valves—exploded, further increasing the reactor core's temperature and pressure.

The Three Mile Island operators did not get the pressure situation under control until fifteen hours after the crisis began. At this point, they turned the primary loop's pumps back on, which resulted in the addition of cooling water that again began circulating around the core. The core's temperature and pressure finally began to decrease. The damage was done, however; half of the power plant's core had become so overheated that it melted down and partially disintegrated. More than 250,000 gallons of highly radioactive water were released from the pressure relief valve system. Amazingly, a complete meltdown of the plant was avoided, but the people of Pennsylvania still had an enormous potential health and environmental problem to contend with—the leakage of radiation into the atmosphere.

3

The Aftermath

One of the things immediately apparent in the aftermath of the Three Mile Island disaster was the potential for human error to result in catastrophe. The two valves that were responsible for controlling the flow of emergency cooling water to the secondary loop had been closed two days prior to the Three Mile Island accident as part of a routine test of the system. It is likely that the valves were accidentally left closed after the system had been tested.

The Official Response

Response to the disaster came immediately from the Nuclear Regulatory Commission's regional office in King of Prussia, Pennsylvania, which alerted NRC headquarters in Washington, D.C. Teams of NRC inspectors were flown to Harrisburg and were soon joined by inspectors and other experts from the United States Department of Energy and the Environmental Protection Agency (EPA). President Carter declared the Three Mile Island site off-limits to

A civil defense worker checks radiation levels as schoolchildren are evacuated in Harrisburg, Pennsylvania, after the accident at Three Mile Island.

all but essential personnel at 11:00 AM on March 28. The atmosphere above the plant was being tested for radioactivity by the next afternoon.

Low levels of radioactive gas that could not be contained had indeed leaked and were detected in the environment. By Friday of that week, Richard Thornburgh, the governor of Pennsylvania, ordered an evacuation of all children and pregnant women who lived within the five-mile zone surrounding Three Mile Island. Furthermore, Thornburgh suggested that people living within ten miles of TMI stay inside and keep their windows and doors sealed. This did little to calm the public's fears; eventually more than 140,000 people fled the

Wednesday, March 28

1:50 PM

A bubble of hydrogen explodes in the reactor's containment building. With pumps again shut off, the core becomes partly uncovered.

area (although most of the people living within that five-mile danger zone would return to their homes by the next week).

During the height of the crisis at Three Mile Island, when there were mistaken fears that a hydrogen bubble that had formed in the reactor's core would mix with oxygen and cause an enormous explosion, President Carter arrived at the Harrisburg airport in an attempt to calm the town's—and the nation's—fears. After being briefed on the gravity and danger of the situation, President Carter decided to enter the plant anyway. He was led right into the plant's control room where high radiation readings had been recorded. This brave gesture—coupled with the discovery that same day that the hydrogen bubble posed no danger—did much to reassure the country. The reactor core had stabilized, and residents began returning home after being assured that only a very small and harmless amount of radiation had been released into the atmosphere.

Negative Health Effects?

Nevertheless, the American public's confidence in the safety of nuclear fuel declined sharply following the TMI accident. For nearly two decades after the Three Mile Island partial nuclear meltdown, the Pennsylvania Department of Health maintained a registry of over 30,000 people who lived within five miles of TMI at the time of the accident. In 1997, the registry was abandoned because no negative patterns in health effects were found. Studies of radiological consequences of the nuclear accident were also conducted by the NRC, the EPA, the United States Department of Energy, the state of Pennsylvania, and the United States Department of Health, Education and Welfare (now known as the Department of Health and Human Services). After the accident, more than a dozen independent studies were also conducted to test the effect on public health. All these studies have supported the findings of the Pennsylvania Department of Health that the people who lived and worked closest to TMI suffered no short- or long-term ill health as a result of the accident.

President Jimmy Carter and First Lady Rosalynn Carter tour Three Mile Island's control room on April 1, 1979. The president's visit reassured the public that the facility and its surroundings were not contaminated by high levels of radiation.

Although no negative health consequences could be directly correlated to the TMI accident, the public continued to raise questions about the possible negative effects of nuclear radiation on human, animal, and plant life. Thousands of samples from the area—of air, water, vegetation, and soil—were collected and tested by various environmental groups. Very low levels of radioactivity could be attributed to the accident. However, it seems that, as a result of all of these investigations and despite the serious damage to the nuclear reactor itself, most of the radiation was contained within the TMI facility, and the negative effects on individuals or the environment was small.

Richard Thornburgh: Pennsylvania Governor

"I first learned of the accident on Wednesday morning, March 28, 1979, at about ten minutes before 8:00 when I received a phone call from our director of emergency management. My first thought was that even though I knew little of nuclear technology, no accident at a nuclear plant could be anything but serious . . . As a result of TMI, my level of skepticism about nuclear power was substantially raised and, like most Americans, I no longer took for granted the fact that this source of electric power was as risk-free as its promoters had indicated in early years."

From *The Washington Post*'s live discussion, "Governing in a Nuclear Crisis"

A worker in a radiation suit inspects a contaminated area of Three Mile Island.

Cleanup

Cleanup, however, was another story entirely. Much like the disaster itself, the cleanup process was very dangerous. All surfaces in the plant had to be decontaminated to prevent possible radioactive exposure. One of the first steps in the cleanup process was to sever TMI-2's connection to TMI-1, so that TMI-1 could continue to operate. Lead bricks were brought in to build a protective wall around the reactor. Nearly 100 tons of radioactive fuel, debris, and water were removed from the TMI-2 reactor. Only after all of the hydrogen was drained from the system could the reactor be shut down, about a month after the accident. The cleanup of the damaged reactor took almost twelve years, as well as the skills of more than 1,000 hazard workers, and cost nearly $1 billion. Cleanup was completed in 1993.

4

Changes in Law and Industry

In 1979, as a result of the Three Mile Island accident, the nuclear energy industry created a self-governing body, the Institute of Nuclear Power Operations, to address issues of public safety and the performance of nuclear power plants. One would think that after a disaster like Three Mile Island, governmental regulations applying to the safe use of nuclear power would become even stricter. Instead, in October 1981, the new United States president, Ronald Reagan, reversed a decision made by President Jimmy Carter in 1977—the one that banned the use of cheap, but dangerous, reprocessed or "used" nuclear fuel.

Even more alarming to those opposed to nuclear power, in 1983 the Reagan administration fought to create the Nuclear Waste Policy Act. The act was intended to help pay for storage facilities for highly radioactive waste. Although nuclear waste certainly had to be put somewhere, earmarking these dollars for that purpose made it clear that the use of nuclear fuel was a permanent part of the nation's current and future energy picture. The act laid out a schedule for moving nuclear waste to permanent underground storage facilities.

A Deadly Nuclear Accident

The potential dangers of nuclear power were again vividly illustrated on April 26, 1986. Explosions during a routine system test at the Chernobyl nuclear reactor near Kiev, Ukraine, in the former Soviet Union, ruptured the power plant's fuel-containment structure and resulted in an immense fire. Extremely high levels of radioactive emissions were released into the atmosphere, spreading over a large swath of territory.

The incident at Chernobyl is considered to be the worst nuclear accident in history. More than 75 million people were exposed to dangerously toxic levels of radiation as a result of the Chernobyl disaster. Just four months later, in August 1986, Soviet doctors were predicting that at least 30,000 cancer-related deaths would occur over the next half-century as a result of the nuclear fallout of the Chernobyl explosion.

Wednesday, March 28	Pumps are again turned on and water begins to flow, cooling the dangerously overheated core. The immediate crisis is over.
3:08 PM	

The Chernobyl disaster made many people question the future use of nuclear energy in the United States. In May 1988, New York governor Mario Cuomo made an agreement with the Long Island Lighting Company (LILCO) to shut down the Shoreham, Long Island, nuclear power plant and dismantle its system. This was a very expensive safety measure—$5.3 billion was lost in investment, wages, and future profits—and the cost was absorbed by LILCO investors, Long Island electricity consumers, and taxpayers nationwide. More than a decade later, LILCO customers are still charged among the highest utility rates in the country, all because of the huge financial loss resulting from the closing of Shoreham.

Engineers at the Chernobyl nuclear power plant in the Ukraine stand at their stations moments after the plant's third reactor was shut down on December 15, 2000, officially closing the plant that caused the world's worst nuclear accident.

After Chernobyl

In October 1992, President George Herbert Walker Bush signed the Energy Policy Act, a law that was meant to map the future energy needs of the United States and provide a blueprint for meeting them. What President Bush sought to do was standardize the operation and licensing of power plants, hoping that devastating malfunctions of the kind seen at Three Mile Island and Chernobyl would decrease. The process for applying for a license to build

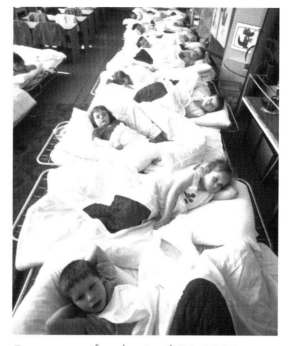

Four years after the April 26, 1986, Chernobyl accident, these young patients filled a hospital ward in Syekovo, a village near the Chernobyl nuclear plant. They were suffering from intestinal problems due to exposure to radiation.

a new plant was also changed so that public advocacy and environmental groups would have more opportunity to be involved in decisions about a proposed plant's size and location. While this law was designed to reduce the many concerns and fears associated with nuclear energy, it also signaled that nuclear power was here to stay, despite its great risks.

Conclusion

Today, the second unit of the Three Mile Island nuclear power plant (TMI-2) has been permanently shut down, with absolutely no plans to reopen.

Its new owner, General Public Utilities Nuclear Corporation, has put most of the parts from TMI-2 into storage. The operating license for TMI's first unit, TMI-1, expires in 2014. At that time, the entire plant will be removed completely, and all of its remaining parts and nuclear waste will be put into permanent storage as well.

Although the accident happened long ago, Three Mile Island continues to be discussed and debated even today.

The disaster at the plant changed the way the public viewed nuclear energy. People became far more skeptical of the limitless and safe uses of nuclear fuel. Not a single new nuclear power plant has been ordered in the United States since the accident at Three Mile Island (though several that had been ordered before the accident have since been built and put into operation). In order to address the public's fears and concerns, the Nuclear Regulatory Commission was forced to change and strengthen the ways in which nuclear power plants are operated. Some of the major changes include:

- A more frequent and regular analysis of the performance of nuclear power plants by NRC management. These senior staffers identify the plants that need additional safety measures, stricter regulations, and greater oversight.

- Greater government regulation of everything from plant design and operation to nuclear fuel transportation and disposal. Power plant operators would have to obey these strict rules and regulations when building and operating their plants.

- Changes to the NRC's inspector programs, such as the practice of hiring inspectors who live in the same town where the plant is located and who work exclusively at that plant. This allows the inspectors immediate access and almost daily inspection of the facility and equipment, as well as a more personal stake in the plant's safety.

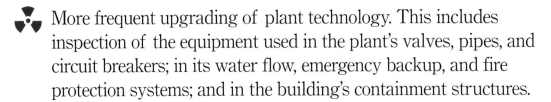

More frequent upgrading of plant technology. This includes inspection of the equipment used in the plant's valves, pipes, and circuit breakers; in its water flow, emergency backup, and fire protection systems; and in the building's containment structures.

The construction of safety barriers to contain radiation in an emergency. Each plant must contain three physical barriers to prevent radiation leaks: nuclear fuel pellets are sealed within steel rods, the steel rods are sealed within a thick steel container, and the container is sealed within a huge concrete and steel structure with walls that are several feet thick.

Despite lingering public fears and doubts about the safety of nuclear energy, it would seem that the government is committed to its continued use and development. In anticipation of a new energy shortage in the coming years, President George W. Bush has placed a renewed emphasis on the utilization of nuclear power. At the same time, the NRC has been taking steps to modify its early site-approval process as well as regulations for preapproved reactor designs, which should shorten the approval process for new construction of reactors.

Even though the country's faith in it was shaken, nuclear energy never went away after the accident at Three Mile Island. Indeed, looking forward, it seems that its future role in American energy policy will only grow and grow.

Glossary

core   The center of a nuclear power plant's system; it contains the control rods.

decontamination   The removal or attempted removal of radioactive waste from an area, body of water, or person.

element   Any of more than 100 fundamental substances that consist of atoms of only one kind and that singly or in combination constitute all matter.

fossil fuel   A fuel, such as coal, oil, or natural gas, that is formed in the earth from plant or animal remains and used for energy needs.

generator   A machine that converts mechanical energy into electrical energy.

molecule   The smallest particle of a substance that retains all the properties of the substance and is composed of one or more atoms.

nuclear fission   The splitting of an atom's nucleus, resulting in the release of a large amount of energy.

nuclear reactor   A device that creates and sustains nuclear fission, thereby creating nuclear energy.

radiation   Energy that is emitted from the nucleus of an unstable atom as a result of nuclear decay.

turbine   The engine system of a nuclear reactor, activated by water or steam.

For More Information

Organizations

Federal Emergency Management Agency (FEMA)
Federal Center Plaza
500 C Street SW
Washington, DC 20472
(202) 646-4600
Web site: http://www.fema.gov

U.S. Department of Energy
1000 Independence Avenue SW
Washington, DC 20585
(800) DIAL-DOE (342-5363)
Web site: http://www.energy.gov

U.S. Nuclear Regulatory Commission
Office of Public Affairs
Washington, DC 20555
(800) 368-5642
Web site: http://www.nrc.gov

Videos

NOVA: Sixty Minutes to Meltdown. WGBH Educational
Foundation, 1983.

Web Sites

Due to the changing nature of Internet links, the Rosen Publishing
Group, Inc., has developed an online list of Web sites related to the
subject of this book. This site is updated regularly. Please use this
link to access the list:

http://www.rosenlinks.com/wds/mtmi/

For Further Reading

Condon, Judith. *Chernobyl and Other Nuclear Accidents.* New York: Raintree/Steck-Vaughn, 1998.

Daley, Michael J. *Nuclear Power: Promise or Peril?* Minneapolis, MN: Lerner Publishing Group, 1996.

Galperin, Anne L. *Nuclear Energy, Nuclear Waste.* Broomall, PA: Chelsea House Publishers, 1992.

Hampton, Wilborn. *Meltdown: A Race Against Nuclear Disaster at Three Mile Island: A Reporter's Story.* Cambridge, MA: Candlewick Press, 2001.

Kidd, J. S., and Renee A. Kidd. *Quarks and Sparks: The Story of Nuclear Power.* New York: Facts on File, 1999.

Stephens, Mark. *Three Mile Island.* New York: Random House, 1980.

Bibliography

Cantelon, Philip L. *The American Atom: A Documentary History of Nuclear Policies from the Discovery of Fission to the Present.* Philadelphia, PA: University of Pennsylvania Press, 1992.

CNN.com. "Three Mile Island, 20 Years Later." March 28, 1999. Retrieved October 2001 (http://www.cnn.com/US9903/28/3mile.anniversary).

Hewlett, Richard G., and Oscar E. Anderson Jr. *History of the U.S. Atomic Energy Commission, Vol. I: The New World, 1939–1946.* Berkeley, CA: University of California Press, 1991.

Hodgson, Peter E. *Nuclear Power, Energy, and the Environment.* London,: Imperial College Press, 1999.

Rees, Joseph V. *Hostages of Each Other: The Transformation of Nuclear Safety Since Three Mile Island.* Chicago, IL: University of Chicago Press, 1996.

Washingtonpost.com. "Twenty Years Later: A Nuclear Nightmare in Pennsylvania." March 27, 1999. Retrieved October 2001 (http://www.washingtonpost.com/wp-srv/national/longterm/tmi/tmi.htm).

WPBS. "American Experience–Three Mile Island." 1999. Retrieved October 2001 (http://www.pbs.org/wgbh/amex/three/index.html).

Wood, M. Sandra, and Suzanne M. Shultz, eds. *Three Mile Island.* Westport, CT: Greenwood Publishing Group, 1988.

World Nuclear Association. "The Accident at Three Mile Island." Retrieved October 2001 (http://www.uilondon.org/safety/tmi.htm).

Index

About the Author

Susie Derkins is a folk artist who lives in New York City.

Photo Credits

Cover, pp. 4–5, 29 © Wally McNamee/Corbis; p. 7 © Frank Hoffman, DOE/Timepix; p. 13 © WGBH Educational Foundation; pp. 16, 20 © Bettmann/Corbis; pp. 18, 25, 36, 37 © AP/Wide World Photos; p. 31 © Dirck Halstead/Timepix; p. 33 © Pennsylvania State University Engineering Library.

Series Design and Layout

Les Kanturek